Interesting Times
TheTrump Presidency

A Chinese Curse;
"May you live in interesting times."

COVID-19, Pandemic,
The Trump Presidency
Debt Default?, Survival.

By: B. J. Galt

Title ID:
Interesting Times
TheTrump Presidency

Amazon Paperback
ISBN: 9798657020014

Email request a PDF
Of this book from
bjongalt@gmail.com

This book; "INTERESTING TIMES, The TRUMP PRESIDENCY" is the end considerations of over 50 Years of political and corporate observation and study.
It addresses key questions:
The Trump Presidency &   COVID-19 Pandemic, Racist Revolt, Rioting & Looting, Big Tech Socialism, Considerations &Conclusions.

What makes the US the most powerful and successful nation in the world?
Why is it threatened with national default and financial ruin? What "recurrence to Constitutional principles" can save it?

America represents a unique, shining example in government. Its success is the envy of people all over the world. The concepts of limited government and freedom to pursue happiness as defined in the US Constitution create powerful forces that generate unprecedented economic prosperity that is far greater than any other nation. American GDP is greater than China, Japan, the UK and Germany combined.

Many countries depend on America for economic, charitable and military support. America is truly Atlas to the World!

When faced with a growing, $Multi Trillion, unsustainable, national debt; Will Atlas America be forced to shrug? Much the Federal Government does is not authorized in the Constitution.

After National Debt default, how can a transition be made to a surviving Constitutional America? A state approved Federal Limit Amendment is proposed to make America fiscally sound, and constitutional again.

To Change America, Big Tech Socialism

<u>**Changing America ; One Party Rule, Big Tech Socialism**</u>

Democrats easily won President & Senate elections in 2020. This proves that Mass, Universal, Unsolicited, Unverifiable Mail In-Ballots & vote manipulation can be used to elect the **least qualified candidates.**

Then, elections cannot be won based on best character & ideas.

Democrat control of the Presidency & both Houses will protect such mail-in ballot voting procedures & strengthen one party rule.

Big Tech Billionaire funding of Democrats and banning Trump & Conservative voices on social media (Twitter, Facebook & Google, etc.) will make The Republican Party irrelevant.

Joe Biden admitted he had: "the most extensive and inclusive voter fraud organization". He validated it with the weakest Presidential Campaign ever which produced 80 Million votes, the largest total ever. Proof of an illegal election.

Democrats easily winning President & Senate elections in 2020 prove that Universal Unsolicited, Unverifiable Mail In Ballots and vote manipulation can be used to elect the <u>least qualified candidates</u>. Voting procedures were used that were <u>not authorized by State Legislatures</u> as required by the US Constitution. Such elections were not legal.

With a Democrat President, Senate & House, legislation will be passed that will ensure even more Democrat favored, future elections.
Big Tech Billionaire funding of Democrats and deletion of Trump & Conservative voices on social media (Twitter, Facebook & Google, etc.) will make The Republican Party irrelevant in future elections.

Creating a Changed America ;
One party rule, Technical Socialism

State Courts including the Supreme
Court refused to rule on these massive,
unlawful elections.

State Legislators ignored their
Constitutional duties to establish
and administer election laws letting
others define how these laws are
interpreted and executed.

The US Congress, intimidated by
Capital rioting, failed to object
to improperly authorized Electors.

With no apparent way to correct a
fraudulent election, 75 Million
disenfranchised Trump voters are told
accept a Biden Presidency. "Don't worry,
be happy."

Ben Franklin warned:
What kind of government have you
given us? He said;
"A Republic, if you can keep it."

Viruses, Lockdowns, Masks, distancing & Vaccinations

CDC reports No Flu in 2020. Flu's Counted as COVID?

Millions of HEALTHY PEOPLE are tested. PCR testing has a HIGH FALSE POSITIVE TEST RATE. Should test only when COVID symptoms are present.

FEW deaths are from COVID only. Invalid, cumulative, COVID Case & Death counts are often repeated to increase COVID fear.

Flu kills more children than COVID.

COVID is an upper respiratory virus disease. Odds of getting it = .0006%. Likely recovery without hospital care 99%.

Most COVID is spread in locked down homes 74% Restaurants / Bars 1.4%.

Masks & Social Distancing do little but create and validate fear.

Stay home when sick. Do not mask and distant healthy people.

LOCKDOWNS do not stop COVID spread. But they do prolong epidemics by preventing immunity development.

Worse, they close schools damaging children, destroy businesses, jobs & stop critical preventive & needed heath care.

The cry of a dying society; STOP SAVING ME!

To end COVID and **to avoid spreading it**: People who test positive with any COVID Symptoms; Fever, cough or sneezing, **should stay at home.**

Two healthy people meet. One wears a mask. The other asks "if neither of us has COVID,Why wear a Mask?"

The masked person says, "Because you may be COVID Asymptomatic."

A Political Myth; "Any Healthy people could be Asymptomatic COVID spreaders."

This is cited as the primary reason that **healthy people** must wear masks, socially distance, avoid crowds of all kinds, etc.

Asymptomatic means, **no symptoms; fever, coughing, sneezing**.

With no symptoms, how can COVID be spread by asymptomatic persons?

Follow Science; Population_Immunity ends Epidemics. Isolation Policies prevent Immunity Development & Prolong Epidemics.

We never shut down Businesses, Schools, Masked, Distanced & Quarantined **Healthy People** for any Fu or Virus since 1918.

COVID-19 is a Virus with fewer Children Deaths than the common Flu.

End Political COVID Isolation policies.

NIAID.NIH.GOV:
"Coronaviruses are a large family of viruses
That <u>usually cause mild to moderate upper-
respiratory tract illnesses, like the common
cold.</u> There are hundreds of Coronaviruses.

Most circulate
among animals. Three were more
serious; SARS-CoV 2002, MERS-CoV 2012.
The 3rd is called SARS-CoV-2. 2019
(COVID-19)."

Initially, US Medical Experts
cited <u>data faulty UK Computer
Models</u> predicted <u>2.3 Million deaths.</u>
Used to justify a National Economic Lock
Down.

Few of **the** Total Population get
the Virus. 99% of
those Recover without medical
treatment. **Most** cases experience mild to
moderate or no symptoms and
recover without special treatment and are
unreported

We have a clearly defined population at risk who can be protected with targeted measures.

The Death Rate is less than 0.003% (3 in 1,000) . Most who die are Elderly with other serious medical problems and are often wrongly labeled Caronavirus deaths.

66% of new NY Cases came from Home Shut ins. This means Home Shut In policies are ineffective, dangerous, and unnecessary. Why use them?

Population Immunity ends Pandemics.

Vital population immunity is prevented by Total Isolation policies. Shut Businesses, Stay In Home, Social Distancing, No Crowds, No Congregations, No Travel, No Hand Shakes, Etc. All prevent immunity development and prolong an epidemic.

Unjustified, Ineffective Total Isolation policies also cause loss of life, stress, wrecked livelihoods, substance abuse, domestic violence, suicides, and a damaged economy.

Elderly are locked in homes and not allowed to be with families, or see grand children, often dying alone.

Instead of focusing care and teatment on the ill or vulnerable, the <u>healthy population</u> is subjected toTotal Isolation policies;

Lock Downs, Shut Businesses, Stay In Home, Social Distancing, No Crowds, No Congregations, No Travel, No Hand Shakes, Wearing masks,Etc.

People are dying in greater numbers because other medical care (prevention, heart, cancer, etc) is not getting done. **Allow all Elective Medical Procedures.**

Focus onProtecting older, at-risk people. eliminates hospital overcrowding. **Keep Hospitals from closing.**

Implement prioritized testing for Nursing Home Workers, Health Care Workers, First Responders, and Patients in hospitals with respiratory symptoms or fever.

<u>The Cure is Worse than the Disease.</u>

Over <u>$6 Trillion</u> will be added to the
<u>$25 Trillion</u> National Debt to pay for
COVID-19 economic losses.
(Generational Theft)

10's of Thousands of small businesses will
not recover and their jobs will be lost.

Profit Losses and Shut Down costs will also
<u>reduce State & Federal 2021 tax revenues</u>
creating greater deficits and Federal Debt
<u>next year</u>.

With delayed and ineffective COVID
defensive policies, Democrat Governors and
Mayors lengthened the epidemic chaos to
damage Trump's Economy and prevent his
reelection.

Protests, Rioting and Destruction

Then, to make matters worse, a black man is
murdered by rogue police unleashing
national racial protests.

ANTIFA & Black Lives Matter Anarchists used these protests as an excuse to foment rioting, property destruction and wanton looting.

With delayed and ineffective COVID defensive policies, Democrat Governors and Mayors lengthened the chaos to further damage   Trump's Economy and prevent his reelection.

WEATHER UNDERGROUND'S
REVOLUTIONARY STRATEGY 1960
Is now also used By; ANTIFA &
BLACK LIVES MATTER:

Destroy Capitalism
The Weapon of Choice; Systematic
Racism And Police Racism
Identify the Victim Classes
Organize the Victim Classes
Engage in International Solidarity
With the Global Movement
Attack and Dethrone GOD

MAKE AMERICA CONSTITUTIONAL AGAIN

3 key questions:

What makes   the USA the most powerful and successful nation   in the world?

Why is the USA   threatened with national default and financial ruin?

What "recurrence to Constitutional Principles" can save the USA?

The American Example

America represents a unique,   shining example in government.

Its success is the envy of people

all over the world. World economies

depend on US success.

USA GDP is > China, Japan, UK, Germany combined.

Many countries depend on America for economic,   charitable and military support.

Atlas America

America is truly Atlas to the World!
When faced with a
$25 + Trillion National Debt;
Will Atlas Shrug?

COVID-19 Spending will add $ 3-6 Trillion to The National Debt.

Budgetary Deficit spending adds to the debt every year.

A Federal Debt Default is likely to occur when Debt Interest cannot be funded or low interest seriously impedes Federal Bond funding.

Much the Federal Government does is not authorized in the Constitution.

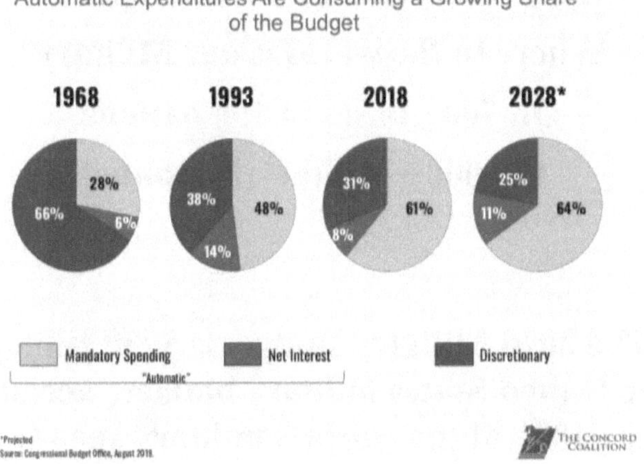

After Debt Default, how can a
transition be made to
a surviving, Constitutional America?

A state approved <u>Federal Limit Amendment</u> is proposed to make America fiscally sound, and constitutional again.

Military Support

Many countries depend on America for military and economic support.

Where in the world is our Military?

On 700+ bases in 150 nations,

170,000+ Military Personnel

The 2020 Military Budget is $730 Billion.
The United States military budget   accounts
for ~40% of the world's military spending.

Loss Of Government Control

**The danger for America is that
people losing control of their
government leads to the creation
of excessive, inefficient, burdensome,
character-crushing government
and personal dependence.**

**How can this be? How can this great
people, possessed of such literacy and
the best communications that
technology can provide, be in danger
losing control of their government?**

**<u>The Federal Government has become
too large to be effectively controlled
through elected representatives.</u>**

Republican Spending;

President Bush added to the problem by never vetoing any Republican spending bill.

Bush authorized the Iraq and Afghanistan wars, the Part D Medication program, the Economic Stimulus Act of 2008 and the TARP bank bailout, all without budgetary funding thereby allowing unprecedented deficits to be created.

The Republicans lost their ideals as a party of small constitutional government and low taxes.

Democrat Spending;
in the first years of the Obama administration, using congressional majorities and the Presidency, the $800 Billion American Recovery and Reinvestment Act of 2009 was passed without funding to stimulate the economy.

This added to the Federal Deficit in that year.   It did little to eliminate the recession. It did increase federal and state spending.

The Affordable Care Act
The Obama administration and Democrat congressional majority passed the 2500 page Affordable Care Act (Obama Care) without any Republican support.

Republicans removed the Obama
Care mandate making it financially
impractical.

Republicans have been unable to pass
federal health alternatives.

Better to use: Direct Primary Care. With
Major Medical (Catastrophic) Insurance
+Tax Free, Health Saving Accounts for
Excellent, Economical, Efficient Health
Care.

Unbalanced Budget Proposals
Democrat or Republican budget
plans only reduce the amount of
budget growth, not current spending.
Future legislators must do
the actual cutting.
None of the plans reduce the
$25 + Trillion current national debt.
Over the next 10 year period,
$7 – 8 Trillion will be added to the debt
<u>not including</u> $6 Trillion COVID-19
spending.

How Long before lack of funding & Interest realities will force insolvency?

How will our children deal with these generational debt burdens?

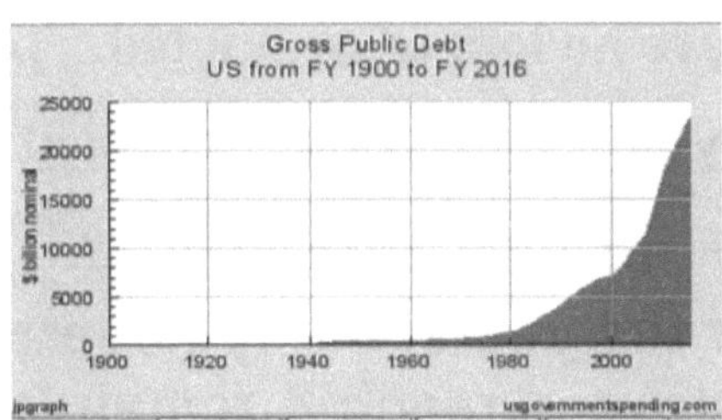

Recent US Federal Deficits Billions
2016: $585,   2017: $666, 2018: $977, 2019 $1 Trillion

Expect to see continuing deficits in the foreseeable future, leading to much more debt. Interest payments on that debt will become the largest item in the federal budget.

<u>The Peter Principle</u>
The Peter Principle states; "In a bureaucracy, everyone tends to rise to their level of incompetence, then they are no longer promoted. <u>In time, every post tends to be occupied by an incompetent employee."</u>

Over the years, many government employees reach & remain at this incompetence level.

<u>A Tipping Point</u>
The critical point is when the number of people living on government entitlements passes 50% and can control future elections.

Today, 45% of US citizens pay no income taxes.

The Democrat party has
support from minorities, welfare
recipients, unions a liberal media and
government workers making it difficult for
anyone to propose any reduction in
government spending or programs.

Constitutional Road Blocks
The Constitution of the United States
is unique among the constitutions of
the world in the way it restricts the
powers of the Federal Government
with checks and balances.

It's allowed powers are specifically
listed in the 10th Amendment which states:
"The powers not delegated to the United
States by the Constitution, nor prohibited
by it to the states, are reserved to the states
respectively, or to the people."

How can this be? How can this great people possessed of such literacy and the best communications that technology can provide be in danger of losing control of their government?

The government has become too large to be effectively controlled through elected representatives because it has strayed from its founding principles. It is now an enormous conglomerate acting as the nation's largest debtor, creditor, property owner, tenant, insurer, health care provider and pension Guarantor.

Government,   A Dangerous Force

George Washington said many years ago: *"Government is not reason, it is not eloquence. It is a force. Like fire, it is a dangerous servant and a Fearful master"*.

National Length Of Life

"The average length of life of 20   once free nations has been just two hundred years. They have gone from liberty to;

abundance; from abundance to complacency; from complacency to apathy; from apathy to dependency; and, from dependency into bondage."

America is 240+ years old.

At the apathy stage?

A Temporary Democracy?

"A democracy is always temporary in nature; it   simply cannot exist as a permanent form of   government."

"A democracy will continue to exist until the   voters discover that they can vote themselves generous gifts from the public treasury. From then on, the majority always votes for the candidates who promise the most benefits which expands the government leading to fiscal insolvency."

A Tipping Point

The critical point is when the number
of people living on government
entitlements passes 50% and
can control future elections.

Or when the National Debt can no
longer be financed.

Today, 45% of US citizens pay no
income taxes.

Consider the current $25 + Trillion
National Debt and continuing annual
deficits along with all the unfunded
liabilities. Actual inability to finance
the National Debt, insolvency, is a
real possibility.

Constitutional Road Blocks

The Constitution of the United States

Is unique among the constitutions
of the world in the way it was written
to restrict the powers
of the Federal Government with
checks and balances.

The Key To American Success

The Constitution of the United States
more severely limits the powers and
extent of the Federal Government
than any ever has before.

It is this restraint of government,
combined with resulting freedom and
incentives for the individual and
businesses that have caused this
country to achieve the success it has.

Control Of Growth

Unfortunately, it is clear that the checks
and balances are not functioning as
intended by the Constitutional Authors.

The Federal Government is now a
massive complex with incomprehensible,
duplicate, extensive powers.

The Federal Register indicates there are over 430 departments, agencies, and sub-agencies in the federal government."

The expansive forces within this massive conglomerate in combination with the beneficiaries of its programs and influences represent explosive potentials for government growth.

Growth Of Federal Government

In the past 10 years the Federal work force has grown from 1,900,000 to 2,400,000. This does not include 500,000+ postal employees.

During this time, Federal employee pay has increased by 129% compared to 74%for private sector workers.

America went off the Gold Standard in 1944. No more conversion of $ to gold is allowed after 1971.

Now the Federal Reserve prints money to fund growing annual US Deficits which causes Dollar Purchasing Power Devaluation

This chart shows $ devaluation up to the year 2013. How much more has the Federal Reserve devalued the dollar with Quantitative Easing (printing money) since then?

Loss Of Monetary Significance

Citizens today have lost a sense of monetary significance, especially when hearing politicians explain spending facts.

Their perceptions of the dimensions and amounts of money actually involved with monetary terms such as; Millions, Billions, or Trillions are often meaningless or unrealistic.

Physical Dimensions Of Money

Not too long ago, $ 1 Billion ($ One Thousand Million) was the maximum sum used to describe spending. Even

$ 1 Billion is not clearly understood by most people.

$1 Billion =   A stack of $1 bills 75 Miles high.

$1 Trillion = One Thousand Billions.

Politicians should not be allowed to state

expenditures in Trillions of Dollars.

The next time you hear politicians speak of Billion and Trillion dollar budgets and expenditures, consider the physical dimensions of the money they are proposing to spend.

When a politician proposes to spend $1 Billion for a project, ask if it is worth 1,000 Million Dollars?

See if the answer shows a clear understanding what a Billion Dollars truly represents.

Enough money has been spent on recent
conflicts to retire all Student loan
debt in America. Yet the world is less
stable today.

Evaluations And Reevalutations

The historian Mommson said 60 years ago about the USA:

"With more than two thousand years of European experience before your eyes, you have repeated every one of Europe's mistakes. "

How many more mistakes have we made during the last sixty years?

Benjamin Franklin was even more pessimistic when he predicted that the Federal Union:¨

"Can only end in despotism as other forms have done before it when the people shall become so corrupt as to need despotic government, being Incapable of any other."

Reevaluation

These are bleak words indeed from these great men.

If our founding principles cannot be made to work. If our people cannot make sound readjustments and maintain effective control of their government, <u>then there is no government system known to mankind that will not eventually be destroyed by its negligent society.</u>

IMMIGRATION CONTROL

In 1970, over 60 percent of American adults were middle-class.

with 62 percent of the   national income.

By 2015, American middle-class,

households collected only 43

percent of the national income,

while the share for the rich surged from 29 percent to almost 50 percent.

For decades,
ever-increasing immigration has
been endorsed by
both political parties. In 1970,
less than 5 percent of America's population
were immigrants. By 2018, that number
had risen to nearly 14 percent.
Democrats know immigrants vote
overwhelmingly   Democratic. Republican
donors want lower wages. They
know immigrants from the third world
will work for less.
More than 15 million illegal
immigrants have been allowed to enter the
United States, get jobs, and use
public services.
Border walls are needed
but cannot completely control thousands of
miles of border.
They are a valuable deterrent for
immigration control

<u>**The most effective solution to the illegal immigration problem is to eliminate the illegal immigrant job magnet by providing employers the means to accurately identify illegal employees and to penalize businesses that still knowingly hire illegal aliens**</u>.

U. S. law requires companies to employ only individuals who may legally work in the United States – either U.S. citizens, or foreign citizens who have the necessary authorization.

Enforce this law. Fine those employers who hire non-verifiable, illegal aliens.

E-Verify is an Internet-based system that allows businesses to determine the eligibility of their employees to work in the United States. E-Verify is fast, free and easy to use and it's the best way employers can ensure a legal work force.

E-Verify, is available to Computer Check for legal immigrant status. Use E-Verify and require, under penalty, legal status in applications for:

Employment, Health Care, Food Stamps, Education, Welfare, Driver License, etc.

Ensure that only <u>authorized</u> citizens can get jobs or benefits. Provide temporary work permits for needed immigrant workers.

Then there will be no reason to illegally immigrate. Jobs and benefits will be limited.

Resident illegal immigrants will be forced to self deport. Immigration Control and Enforcement (ICE) can provide assistance for deportment.

This will also deter Visa Overstays.

Elimination of illegal Immigration labor is even more critical with 10's of Millions of US citizens unemployed due to pandemic Lock Downs.

The concept of Sanctuary Areas that protect illegal criminals from being deported by ICE will also be unnecessary and can be eliminated.

By eliminating immigrant job potentials and any support systems that encourage them, they will return to their country. They can choose to utilize legal, merit based, immigration processes to come to America and become legitimate citizens.

ELIMINATE GUN FREE ZONES

Stop labeling GUN FREE ZONES.
They identify A Soft Target.
Label <u>all potential targets</u> as

GUN PROTECTED ZONES

Gun Free Zones   Attract Terrorists and   Shooters.   Because, likely there will be No return Fire in Gun Free Zones. Police will be too late to prevent killings.

The <u>Possible or   ACTUAL</u> presence of Trained Gun Carriers discourages and stops Shooters. Fewer deaths are likely if Trained Gun Carriers can return fire.   GUN PROTECTED ZONE Signs deter and discourage would be Terrorists and Mass Shooters.

Label all potential target zones to deter and discourage attackers. These GUN PROTECTED ZONE labels are available on EBAY.

Concealed Weapons Carry
A Crime and   Terrorism Attack Defense.

The best defense against crime and mass   shootings is a populace with a significant number of people carrying concealed weapons. The police seldom respond quick enough while such crimes are being committed.

The ability to defend in real-time is critical .   Concealed carry defenders in mass shooting situations become critical to provide immediate efforts to stop the shooters and minimize loss of life.

Mass shootings by a deranged individual or a few terrorists, can kill many helpless people before police can arrive. The presence of concealed carry defenders in mass shooting situations become critical to provide immediate efforts to stop the shooters and minimize loss of life.

Mass shootings occur in Gun Free Zones because the perpetrators know there will be little defense to their attacks in such soft target places. There will also likely be time to do serious damage before police are likely to arrive.

Signs denoting a Gun Free Zone should be eliminated. Concealed Weapon carrying should also be promoted. Where this is done, crime rates are significantly lower. In past mass shootings, the presence of persons carrying concealed weapons would likely have saved many lives.

Recurrence To Principles

In Article 15 of the Virginia Declaration of Rights, which was drafted and adopted in 1776, there appears this statement:

"No free government or the blessings of liberty can be preserved to any people but by firm adherence to justice, moderation, temperance, frugality, and virtue and by <u>frequent recurrence to fundamental principles.</u>"

Political Parties

Theodore Roosevelt had this to say about political parties in his day:

"The old parties are husks, with no real soul within either, divided   on artificial lines, boss-ridden and privilege-controlled, each a jumble of incongruous elements, and neither daring to speak out wisely and fearlessly on what should be said on the vital issues of the day."

This could be descriptive of the Republican and Democrat parties today.

The 2012 presidential Election

The Reelection of President Obama gave him the ability to:

Fully implement the Affordable Health Care law (Obama Care).

Better to use: Direct Primary Care. With Major Medical (Catastrophic) Insurance +Tax Free, Health Saving Accounts for Excellent, Economical, Efficient Health Care.

Obama appointed two Supreme Court justices. ensuring Progressive (Liberal) support for constitutional rulings.

The 2016 Election of Trump

Trump redefined political standards, conventions and conduct to the dismay and opposition of both the political parties, government bureaucracies, liberal medias and academia.

He accomplished much in spite of opposition from all these groups and a Democrat House Of Representatives.

In 2016, Trump registered as a Republican. He actually   registered as a Republican in 1987 and since has changed his party affiliation five times.

In 1999, Trump changed his party affiliation to the **Independence Party of New York**. In August 2001, Trump changed his party affiliation to Democratic.

In September 2009, Trump changed his party affiliation back to the Republican Party. In December 2011, Trump changed to "no party affiliation" (independent). In April 2012, Trump again returned to the Republican Party.

Although Trump was the Republican nominee, he has noted that the official 2016 Republican National Convention, diverges from his own views.

In February 2017, Trump stated that he was a "total nationalist" in a "true sense". In October of 2018, Trump again described himself as a nationalist.

In 2016, it is remarkable how the ruling class responded to his election.

Trump won the general election with Electoral Votes. When Trump assumed office, the permanent Republican & Democrat bureaucrats, (Deep State), in Washington and Media worked to sabotage his administration:

Mueller Report: The Investigation into Russian Interference in the 2016 Presidential Election

It's the conclusion of 23 months, 34 indictments and guilty pleas, 500 search warrants and 2,300 subpoenas and $30+ Million cost that there was no Russian Collusion or Obstruction of Justice.

Then, an Impeachment attempt

failed in the Senate.

In spite of Democrat and biased media opposition, Trump has accomplished much that would appeal to conservative politicians with tax cuts and the elimination of many regulations.

Conservatism

Roget's International Thesaurus lists the following as being synonymous with "Conservative":

"Unprogressive, reactionary, rightist, right winger, die hard, bitter ender, stand patter, uncompromiser, irreconcilable, intransigent, old fogey, stick in the mud, moss back, hard shell, long hair and, old school."

These are hardly proper words to use to describe positive American philosophies of freedom and limited government.

Synonymous with Liberal (now termed Progressive) is:

progressive, reactionary, open-minded, generous, broad-minded, moderate, free-thinking, tolerant, progressive, protective, etc.

Liberals tend to favor government solutions and bigger government. The term "Liberal" has lost favor recently. So the term "Progressive" is now used more commonly to describe what Liberal used to define.

Effective Efficient Government Constitutional and Independent

1. Must be efficiently responsive to valid functional needs at state and federal levels.

 2. It must establish and retain functions at the lowest appropriate level of control.

3. It must be self disciplining with effective oversight, and operational checks and balances.

 4. .It must possess effective processes of periodic function review, rejustification and adjustment.

 5. It must be, Constitutionally authorized to be fiscally responsible and controlled.

How To Survive

The best potentials for eliminating deficits and reducing the debt to avoid national insolvency is to support:

Elimination or return of unconstitutional federal spending to the states.

Promote   powerful growth of the national economy.

These must be supported by tax reform and regulation policies that will generate economic expansion.

To Reestablish Constitutional Government:

A FEDERAL LIMIT AMENDMENT

The total annual expenditures of the Federal Government of the United States shall not exceed a limit established at the time of ratification of this amendment except as may be authorized at any time for periods of up to twelve months by at least fifty one percent of State Legislatures. After ratification of this amendment, all income of the Federal Government of the United States in excess of the established expenditure limit shall be disbursed to the States on the basis of population or shall be used to reduce the national debt.

Basic disciplines would be created by such an Amendment:

1. Control of the size and growth of the Federal Government through constitutional budgetary restraints.

2. Debt reduction or dispersion of excess federal funds in a manner that is nationally equitable and <u>not subject</u> to federal political influence.

3. Federal competition for available funds within the Federal Limit will increase program oversight, rejustification and the reduction and elimination of unnecessary and duplicate functions.

4. State competition for available funds would add an additional check and balance effect to the Federal Government.

5. The Constitutional Congressional requirement to control the declaration of war would be reinforced.

The Vietnam, Iraq and the 19 + year   Afghanistan wars <u>would likely not have been authorized</u> and continually funded with this amendment in effect.

6. States rights and constitutional federalism would be strengthened. This fact would provide a strong incentive for states to use their constitutional right to institute a Constitutional Convention and pass a Federal Limit Amendment.

The states, in initial agreement, designed, created and ratified the Constitution of the United States.

Ultimately the states must concur in the validity of the US Constitution.

If the Federal Government significantly deviates from the specifications in the Constitution, Article 5 defines the right of states to propose and ratify amendments as needed.

"Amendment ratification by ¾ of the several States or by conventions."

If the Federal Debt is ever to be reduced, the first requirement is to balance the Federal Budget by eliminating the annual deficits.

What is the deficit? It is the amount by which the Federal Government outlays exceeds its total income for a fiscal year. Such deficits are added to the accumulating National Debt.

US Budget Deficit Compared to GDP, Debt Increase, and Events

Fiscal Year	Deficit (in billions)	Debt Increase (by FY)	Deficit /GDP	Events Affecting Deficit
2009	$1,413	$1,632	9.8%	**Stimulus Act·**
2010	$1,294	$1,905	8.6%	**Obama tax cuts· ACA· Simpson-Bowles·**
2011	$1,300	$1,229	8.3%	**Debt crisis·**
2012	$1,087	$1,276	6.7%	**Fiscal cliff·**
2013	$679	$672	4.0%	**Sequester· Government shutdown·**
2014	$485	$1,086	2.7%	**Debt ceiling·**
2015	$438	$327	2.4%	Defense = $736.4 b.
2016	$585	$1,423	3.1%	Defense = $767.3 b.

2017	$665	$672	3.4%	Defense = $812.3 b.
2018 (est)	$833	$1,271	4.0%	Defense = $824.7 b.
2019(est)	$984	$1,187	NA	
2020 (est)	$987	$1,198	NA	

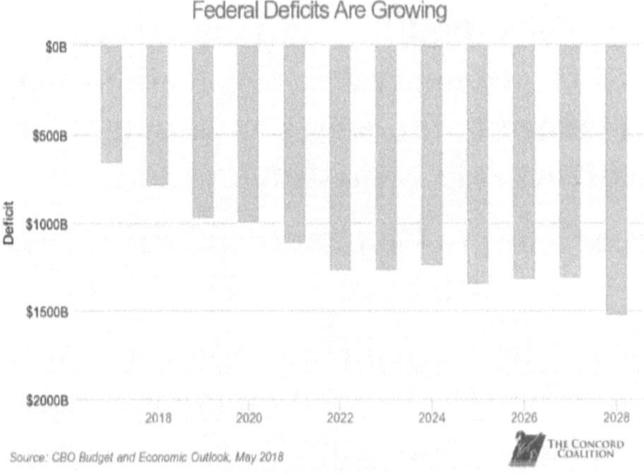

The National Debt will continue to grow as long as deficits continue to add to it.

$ Trillions will be added to compensate for COVID-19 economic losses

The Key Question

The key question is; <u>How can the Federal Budget be balanced and the National Debt reduced?</u>

It will require elimination or reduction of many of the current operations of the Federal Government.

Especially duplicate and unnessesary operations. In many cases, operations may be returned to the States to assume their correct role in these operations.

A recurrence to Constitutional Principles will be required.

<u>National debt default and insolvency will occur when the interest on the national debt or lack of continual funding seriously erodes the funds available to meet national budgetary requirements.</u>

Powerful Potentials For Economic Growth

Energy Economic Potential

Great potential exists in positive expansion of energy resources. The US has the potential to become energy independent and energy rich if national policies and incentives focus on such resources.

Oil, natural gas, coal, nuclear must all be supported and promoted. Solar and wind power generation can also be supported as they develop and become economically competitive.

The Power Of Computing

A force that powerfully strengthens and stimulates the economy is the continuing acceleration of the speed and power of computers.

Gordon Moore, a CEO of the Intel Corporation chip manufacturer stated Moore's Law.

Moore's law is the observation that over the history of computers, the number of transistors on chips doubles approximately every two years.

The first transistors were thumb size.   Today, 4 Billion + transistors exist on the computer chip in a Cell Phone.

Computer chip technology decreased in size and doubled in speed and memory capacity every 2 years.   What is amazing is that this doubling of computer power is likely to continue for the foreseeable future.

The influence of this multiplying computer power has the potential to continue to accelerate the productivity and expansion of the US economy as well as world interconnectivity.

Computer Power Integration

As computing power proliferates and is integrated into products, more control and intelligence will increase their value.

Robotics and 3D printing of parts will become more capable increasing accuracy, speed and productivity thereby vastly improving manufacturing.

As computing power is further integrated into transportation vehicles and roads, safety and efficiencies will be greatly improved.

EXPONENTIAL
COMPUTER DRIVEN LIFE CHANGES

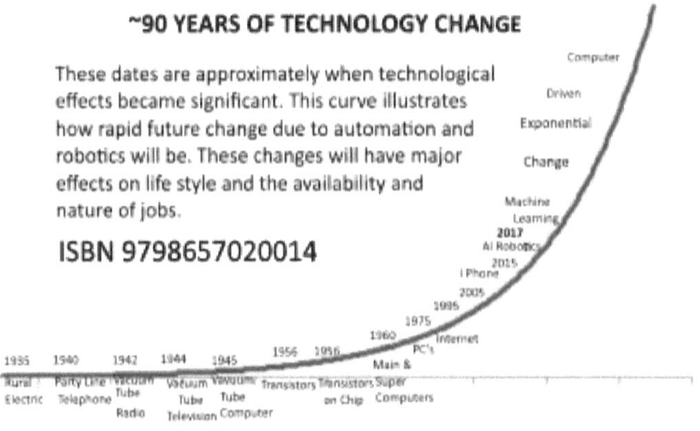

The Greatest Need Today

Examinations and thought which will find ways to effectively perform "recurrence to governmental principles" represent the greatest lack in the present day American political society.

Government must be made more efficient and effectively responsive to needs for all Americans.

Possible Disciplines

Pay-Go policies which require that every new expenditure

must be funded from budget cuts.

Presidential Line Veto to eliminate unjustifiable line item spending

from bills that he signs.

Term limits for representatives to improve government attitudes by removing incentives for career politicians.

Any politician who votes for a budget that exceeds a 3% deficit will not be eligible for reelection.

A Constitutional Amendment to require balanced budgets.

Add "sunset provisions" to laws to force periodic review and

rejustification of need.

<u>A Worthy Goal</u>

<u>Reform of the Federal Government to truly conform to the disciplines of the Constitution.</u>

American principles of freedom have created the greatest, most successful nation in the history of the world.

With effective recurrence to constitutional government, an even better, shining example of an ideal society can be provided to the world.

<u>Instead of Nation Building, let other societies be persuaded and encouraged by a USA excellent, successful national example.</u>

The world is at a medieval stage in terms of

intelligent use and control

of government in society.

Our ability to design and implement new, functional systems of governmental control will determine whether we now move into a dark age of smothering, fiscal bankruptcy, irresponsible, socialistic over-government and an eventual end to the "American Miracle".

Can we evaluate the past and from this evaluation reform the principles of freedom and government thereby giving a new vitality and concern to American politics?

Creative minds that can provide answers to fill the vacuum between right and left extremism constitute this nation's greatest present need.

Hopefully, such a need cannot go unfulfilled.

Our current path of fiscal irresponsibility is leading to a National Debt that is greater than our Annual Gross Domestic Product.

<u>Current and future spending projections could actually lead to national Insolvency.</u>

Low interest rates discourage puchases of Federal Bonds to financeNational Debt

As interest rates rise, the need to pay the rates required to sustain the massive national debt will drastically impact the nation's ability to meet its required expenditures.

<u>Continuing down this path, Atlas America will have to shrug off the weight of the world.   It will have no choice.</u>

What will we pass on to our grandchildren?

Generational Theft and Debt,

Unfillable program promises, massive,

Uncontrollable government and unsustainable national debts?

Will we be easily led down this path?

Will this still be a nation founded on Constitutional principles of effective government in a free society?

Will Abraham Lincoln's description of America having "Government of the people, by the people and for the people" still apply?

With awareness, concern and action it can be so.

Interesting Times
TheTrump Presidency

A Chinese Curse;
"May you live in interesting times."
COVID-19, Pandemic,Meuller,
Impeachment,
Revolt, Racist Rioting, Looting,
Debt Default, Survival

By: B. J. Galt

Who is B. J. Galt?

B. J. Galt is the pseudonym of a retired Computer System Engineer. He has published three books defining how end users can be designers of major applications. He originated the design of the BIS computer software system which was responsible for >$3 Billion in system sales for a major corporation. The BIS Story is Available at Amazon Books:

"Business Information Server, BIS, THE Killer APP"
ASIN: 1502448580

At near 90 Years of age he prefers anonymity in addressing

political matters.

This book addresses 3 key questions:

What makes the USA the most powerful and successful nation   in the world?

Why is it threatened with national default and financial ruin?

What "recurrence to Constitutional principles" can save it?

The author's reflections, concerns and recommendations are based on over 40 years of observance of large, corporate bureaucracy and political, historical research experience. As a past Conservative and Republican, he now describes himself as a "Constitutional Independent".

This book represents his evolved & current, political perspectives. It suggests solutions and initiatives to accomplish
a   return of proper Constitutional powers to the states providing for a Federal Government that is fiscally sound, effective in its operations and responsive to the nation's needs while   restoring liberty to the individual, dignity to the legislature and purpose to the ballot box.

Interesting Times
The Trump Presidency

A Chinese Curse; "May you live in interesting times." : Meuller, Impeachment, COVID-19, Revolt, Debt Default, Survival

By: B. J. Galt

Title ID:

INTERESTING TIMES
TRUMP RESIDENCY

ISBN

Amazon Paperback

ISBN: 9798657020014

:

Email request a PDF
Of this Key Point Book from:
bjongalt@gmail.com